THE

# *DAILY SPARK*

*180 easy-to-use lessons and class activities!*

# THE DAILY SPARK

Critical Thinking
Journal Writing
Poetry
Pre-Algebra
SAT: English Test Prep
Shakespeare
Spelling & Grammar
U.S. History
Vocabulary
Writing

THE

# *DAILY SPARK*

# *Vocabulary*

# Introduction

The *Daily Spark* series gives teachers an easy way to transform downtime into productive time. The 180 exercises—one for each day of the school year—will take students five to ten minutes to complete and can be used at the beginning of class, in the few moments before turning to a new subject, or at the end of class.

The exercises in this book may be photocopied and handed out to the class, projected as a transparency, or even read aloud. In addition to class time use, they can be assigned as homework exercises or extra credit problems.

A command of English vocabulary will help students with everything from standardized tests to paper-writing. The *Daily Spark* makes learning vocabulary fun with fill-in-the-blanks, word games, and humor.

Spark your students' interest with the *English Vocabulary Daily Spark*!

# *evanescent* (adj)

*[handwritten: 9/21/05]*

---

Context clues: *The evanescent mist disappears each day after the sun rises above the city.*

Complete the words to create two synonyms of **evanescent**:

br __*[ief]*__

temp __*[orary]*__

Write a sentence using the word **evanescent**.

*[handwritten: I would like to give you an evanescent test today]*

**1**

# *negligible* (adj)

Context clues: *Such a negligible flaw in the diamond would never be noticed except by a professional.*

Underline the word that does not belong.

TINY        NEGLIGIBLE      ~~MAJOR~~      INSIGNIFICANT

Write a sentence using the word **negligible**.

The family was in a car accident and there was negligible damage.

Hurricane Katrina was not a negligible storm.

2

# *capitulate* (v)

*end. capture*

Context clues: *After enduring a brutal siege, the king's forces army was forced to capitulate.*

In the blanks below, write two synonyms for **capitulate**.

give up   surrender

In the blanks below, write two antonyms for **capitulate**.

keep going   dont stop

Write a sentence using the word **capitulate**.

In the monopay game, Susy had all hotes and Bob had none, so he had to capitulate.

# *incessant* (adj)

Context clues: *Furious about the dog's incessant barking, the neighbor called the police.*

Complete the words to create two synonyms of **incessant**:

conti n u o u s

non s t o p

Write a sentence using the word **incessant**.

The teacher was annoyed at the students incessant talking

# *utopia* (n)

Context clues: *After a harsh winter in North Dakota, Miami seemed like a utopia.*

Write a few sentences describing your own **utopia**.

It would be mountions with great views. There would be a water fall and a lake to swim in. There would also be a lot of open land to play sports in.

# *lethargy* (n)

Context clues: *Mike seems really lethargic; he slept through math today.*

Complete the words to create two antonyms of **lethargy**:

en e r g y

enthus i s i m

Write a sentence using the word **lethargy**.

I stayed up until 6:00 in the morning thats why I'm so lethargy.

# *fluctuate* (v)

Context clues: *My mood is fluctuating wildly today. One minute I'm hugging everyone, and the next minute I'm screaming and crying.*

List three things that **fluctuate**.

your mood
the weather
tempature

# *capricious* (adj)

Context clues: *The capricious actress demanded a bowl of green lollipops in her dressing room, decided she didn't want them, and threw the bowl against the wall.*

Complete the words to create two synonyms of **capricious**.

er <u>a</u>t<u>i</u>t<u>i</u><u>c</u>

wh<u>i</u>m<u>i</u><u>s</u>cal

Write a sentence using the word **capricious**.

The batting order, for the Phillies is always capricious

# *venerate* (v)

Context clues: *The venerated old professor walked onstage to accept the award.*

Eliminate the word that does not belong.

WORSHIP          LIONIZE          ESTEEM          DISGRACE

Write a sentence using the word **venerate**.

I venerate the phillies

# *enigma* (n)

Context clues: *Baffled by the enigma of the missing socks, Angel decided to call in the experts.*

Write a sentence or two about something you consider **enigmatic**.

One thing I find enigmatic is who is going to win the world series this year. Is it Boston? Chicago? New York?

# *pompous* (adj)

Context clues: *Ernesto, the most pompous senior in the entire school, struts around the halls like he's royalty.*

Circle the synonyms of **pompous** and cross out the antonyms of **pompous**.

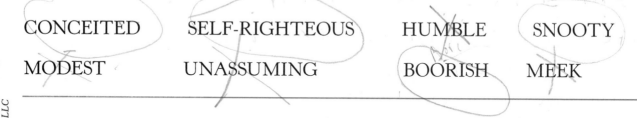

CONCEITED          SELF-RIGHTEOUS          HUMBLE          SNOOTY

MODEST                UNASSUMING                BOORISH          MEEK

# *zenith* (n)

Context clues: *At the zenith of her career, she had over five lucrative endorsement deals and was considered a lock for MVP.*

Complete the words to create two synonyms of **zenith**.

summ_m_i_t_

a_p_e_x

Write a sentence using the word **zenith**.

Jimmy Rollins is at the zenith of his baseball career.

# *clandestine* (adj)

Context clues: *The government agent trained for years before he began his clandestine activities overseas.*

Underline the word that does not belong.

CONSPICUOUS     UNDERGROUND     COVERT     STEALTHY

Write a sentence using the word **clandestine**.

In Harriet the spy Harriet was very clandestine in her spying.

# *fortuitous* (adj)

Context clues: *On his way to the gym, Andrew made a fortuitous discovery: a hundred dollar bill lying on the sidewalk.*

List **fortuitous** events that you've experienced.

In the newspaper one day, it said that Phillies player David Bell has never hit a grand slam and probably never will. That night, it was bases loaded and David Bell hit a grand slam.

# *propensity* (n)

Context clues: *The trophy wife had a propensity for flashy, expensive clothes.*

Complete the words to create two synonyms of **propensity**:

Incl i n a t i o n

Tend a n c y

Write a sentence using the word **propensity**.

Silvi has a propensity for politics and baseball.

15

# *sporadic* (adj)

Context clues: *Beth's sporadic attendance infuriated Coach Maver, who accused her of not truly caring about floor hockey.*

Write a sentence using the word **sporadic**.

Marissa dislikes Bible so she has a sporadic attendance because is the time issue.

# *pragmatic* (adj)

Context clues: *Lucy, always pragmatic, didn't panic when the Winter Dance decorations caught on fire; she simply dialed 911 and instructed everyone to exit the gym calmly.*

Complete the words to create two antonyms of **pragmatic**.

un _realis_ t _i_ c

idea _listic_

Write a sentence using the word **pragmatic**.

_____

# *sycophant* (n)

Context clues: *Bill is such a sycophant. As student council president, all he does is kiss up to the principal and praise all of the vice principal's decisions.*

List three character traits of a person who is **sycophantic**.

flatterer
kisser apple
"Daddys girl"

Write a sentence using the word **sycophant**.

My sister can be so sycophant
sometimes and always gets her way

# *efface* (v)

Context clues: *"Only time will efface my heartbreak,"* Emilie sobbed.

Circle the synonyms of **efface** and cross out the antonyms of **efface**.

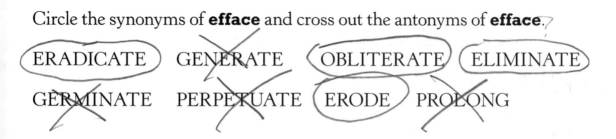

(ERADICATE)   ~~GENERATE~~   (OBLITERATE)   (ELIMINATE)

~~GERMINATE~~   ~~PERPETUATE~~   (ERODE)   ~~PROLONG~~

Write a sentence using the word **efface**.

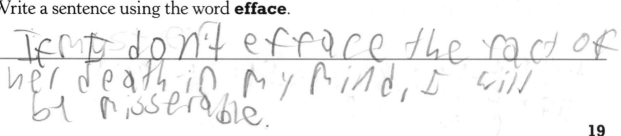

If my don't efface the rad of her death in my mind, I will by misserable.

# *spurious* (adj)

Context clues: *Abe tried to defend himself against spurious accusations that he had rigged the cheerleading competition.*

List as many synonyms of **spurious** as you can. Include slang words.

false
untrue
lie
fake

Write a sentence using the word **spurious**.

In the 10 commandments it says
not to attempt spurious
witness

# *benevolent* (adj)

Context clues: *The benevolent alumnus lavished money on his alma mater, urging the creation of a fund for impoverished applicants.*

Complete the words to create two synonyms of **benevolent**.

gen_ _ _ _s

c_ r_ _g

*[handwritten annotations:]* good, Haverford, Penn, Perelman, Penn, impoverty = poor, application, malevolent = evil

Write a sentence using the word **benevolent**.

*[handwritten:]* My benevolent mother donated a lot of money to project rainbow, a homeless shelter.

# *acquiesce* (v)

Context clues: *After enduring hours of nagging and whining, Mrs. Nixon acquiesced to her son's pleas and gave him a later curfew.*

*time to be home*

Cross out the words that are not synonyms of **acquiesce**.

~~CONSENT~~   ~~DISSENT~~   SUBMIT   AGREE

~~OPPOSE~~   ~~ACCEPT~~   ~~ASSENT~~   CONTEST

*opponents*  *White Sox → Astros*        *ascent*

Write a sentence using the word **acquiesce**.

I will not acquiesce to your request even though your screening incessan

# *partisan* (adj)

Context clues: *Although the president promised to change the tone, the year was characterized by bitter partisan bickering.*

Complete the words to create two antonyms of **partisan**.

imp o r t i a ~~~

neu t r a l

*(bi)*partisan      moderate

Write a sentence using the word **partisan**.

In 2004 My class was mostly
partisan for Ied John kerry
in the election

23

# *candid* (adj)

Context clues: *"Be candid," said Eric. "Do these pants make my thighs look fat?"*

List two situations in which being **candid** could be good, and then list two situations in which being **candid** could be bad.

Write a sentence using the word **candid**.

# *parochial* (adj)

Context clues: *After years of living a sophisticated, liberal life in the city, Ramon found his parents' small-town mindset unbearably parochial.*

Cross out the words that are not synonyms of **parochial**.

CLOSED-MINDED    OPEN-MINDED    UNSOPHISTICATED

SECULAR    INSULAR    NARROW

Write a sentence using the word **parochial**.

# *rhetoric* (n)

*[handwritten: public speaking]*

Context clues: *Claudia is a master of rhetoric. After listening to her for a few minutes, you'll believe whatever she's telling you.*

Complete the words to create two synonyms of **rhetoric**.

ora__tor__y  *[handwritten: tor]*

prop__aga__nd__a__  *[handwritten: aga, a]*

Write a sentence using the word **rhetoric**.

*[handwritten: My mother J really good at rhetoric She goes up infront of many people and talks about the coming election.]*

# *taciturn* (adj)

Context clues: *The taciturn patient spent her time staring at the wall and ignoring her nurses.*

Underline the synonyms of **taciturn** and cross out the antonyms of **taciturn**.

LOQUACIOUS     RESERVED     GARRULOUS     MUTE

RETICENT     TALKATIVE     CHATTY     LONG-WINDED

Write a sentence using the word **taciturn**.

Sometimes she can be taciturn, and others she can be really talkative.

# *irrefutable* (adj)

found guilty

Context clues: *The evidence was irrefutable, and the jury convicted her after only an hour of deliberation.*

thinking

something that can't be debated

List five **irrefutable** facts.

1. Silvi is the oldest child.
2. Hatti is the youngest.
3. You have a dog.
4. You are a girl.

Write a sentence using the word **irrefutable**.

In court since the defendant dened an irrefutable fact, the jury found him guilty.

# *cajole* (v)

Context clues: *After much cajoling and wheedling, Alex managed to get the beauty queen to go on a date with him.*

Complete the words to create two synonyms of **cajole**.

pers u a d e

conv i n c e

Write a sentence using the word **cajole**.

When my dog, Jessi, refuses to come in the house, I cajole her with a treat.

# *iconoclast* (n)

Context clues: *One iconoclast wore jeans to the prom, which enraged the prom committee.*

*[handwritten: POMPUS]*

*[handwritten: mad angry]*

List three famous **iconoclasts**.

Write a sentence using the word **iconoclast**.

*[handwritten: Some iconoclasts are so pompus and they set a bad example to their fans.]*

# *disseminate* (v) *IM'ing email*

Context clues: *The dissemination of information always happened right after school, when groups of friends got together and gossiped about the day's news.*

Cross out the words that are not synonyms of **disseminate**.

BROADCAST     ~~HARVEST~~     DISTRIBUTE     ~~SCATTER~~

~~COLLECT~~     PUBLICIZE     ~~PROTECT~~     PROPAGATE

*Plants — plant — seeds*

Write a sentence using the word **disseminate**.

Every night, I watch the sports channel so I can disseminate what happened to my friends the next day.

# *aloof* (adj)

Context clues: *Unlike the eager and friendly dog, who barked with excitement whenever she saw her owner, the cat was aloof and disliked human company.*

List synonyms for **aloof**.

People - Person

Write a sentence using the word **aloof**.

the new stubant was nervous around her new classmates so she was aloof

# *innate* (adj)

Context clues: *My sledding prowess is a combination of innate ability and dedicated training.*

Complete the words to create two antonyms of **innate**.

lea ⌒n ed

reh e a r sed

Write a sentence using the word **innate**.

I am very innatly good at math.

# *placate* (v)

Context clues: *In an attempt to placate his furious students, Mr. Mallory agreed to rethink his grading policy.*

Complete the words to create two synonyms of **placate**.

soo the

pac ify

Write a sentence using the word **placate**.

My teacher doesn't placate us when were talking, he gives us pink slips

# *fallacy* (n)

Context clues: *A lot of people believe that going outside with wet hair will give you a cold, but that's a total fallacy.*

List five common **fallacies**.

"I didn't do it"    "I didn't say that"
"I'm finished my homework"    "I left my homework
"I don't have any homework"      at home"

Write a sentence using the word **fallacy**.

Middle school is full of drama, gossip and fallacy.

# *magnanimous* (adj)

Context clues: *In a magnanimous gesture, the oil magnate donated five million dollars to a local animal shelter.*

List three people you consider **magnanimous**.

My mom
My dad
My friend Maytal

Write a sentence using the word **magnanimous**.

Maytal was very magnanimous today, she gave me 5 dollars!

# *expedite* (v)

---

Context clues: *In order to expedite the check-in process, please have your ID out.*

Complete the words to create two synonyms of **expedite**.

acc _e_ _l_ _a_ _r_ at _e_

hu _r_ _r_ _y_

Write a sentence using the word **expedite**.

_____

# *salubrious* (adj)

Context clues: *The doctor recommended such salubrious actions as jogging, eating leafy greens, and getting more sleep.*

List five **salubrious** actions. Then list five **insalubrious** actions.

exersizing etledr        watching TV
playing sports           eating junk food
eating salads            sitting all day
eating fruit             eating things off the ground
sleeping                 going outside in the winter with out jacket

Write a sentence using the word **salubrious**.

It is salubrious to wear warm clothes in this type of weather

# *elucidate* (v)

Context clues: *The tutor tried her best to elucidate the algebra concept, but Ben just stared at her with a glazed look in his eyes.*

Underline the word that does not belong.

ILLUMINATE    EXPLAIN    CLARIFY    MUDDLE    EXPOUND

Write a sentence using the word **elucidate**.

The teacher tried hard to elucidate the word 'sililicate' to her students.

# *dulcet* (adj)

Context clues: *In dulcet tones, the sirens lured the sailors to their doom.*

Circle the **dulcet** items and cross out the **clamorous** items.

CYMBALS      BIRDS CHIRPING      LINKIN PARK CONCERT

LULLABY      VIOLINS      BARKING DOGS

*my opinion*

*eva pat*

Write a sentence using the word **dulcet**.

I heared a dulcest sound coming from my sister room, it was her playing violih

VOCABULARY

© 2004 SparkNotes LLC

# *augment* (v)

Context clues: *Ali, determined to augment her Barbie collection, spent every free afternoon searching for new dolls.*

Complete the words to create two synonyms of **augment**.

inc re a se

supp l e men t

Write a sentence using the word **augment**.

Every body I try to agoment the number of pagys Freads in in girls in pants

# *paltry* (adj)

Context clues: *For three years, the castaway survived on paltry amounts of fish, coconut, and bamboo.*

Underline the words that are not similar to **paltry**.

AMPLE    TRIFLING    SCANT    ABUNDANT

SLIGHT    NEGLIGIBLE    PLENTY    SCARCE

Write a sentence using the word **paltry**.

There was a paltry amount of cheesecake left after the party.

# *judicious* (adj)

Context clues: *After making a judicious comparison of both paintings, Mrs. Hubley awarded the blue ribbon to the still life of fried calamari.*

Complete the words to create two synonyms of **judicious**.

shr _ _ _

pr _ d _ _ _

Write a sentence using the word **judicious**.

_____

# *perfunctory* (adj)

Context clues: *After delivering a perfunctory greeting to her assembled aunts and uncles, Alexis slunk out of the room and went looking for her cousins.*

List five jobs, chores, tasks, or assignments you perform in a **perfunctory** manner. setting the table
reading
writing
walting the dog

Write a sentence using the word **perfunctory**.

# *winsome* (adj)

Context clues: *Julia treated the handsome checkout guy to a winsome smile.*

Cross out the words that are not synonyms of **winsome**.

ENDEARING ~~REVOLTING~~ ~~OBNOXIOUS~~ APPEALING

ENGAGING AMIABLE CHARISMATIC COMPELLING

Write a sentence using the word **winsome**.

She gave a winsome smile to the
teacher, to be on her good side

# *homogeneous* (adj)

Context clues: *The student body at the state college is totally homogeneous; everyone looks like they've just stepped out of a J. Crew catalog.*

Complete the words to create two synonyms of **homogeneous**.

uni _f_rm

id_e_nt_i_ca_l_

Write a sentence using the word **homogeneous**.

Every one got a homogeneous grade on their test

# *omnivorous* (adj)

Context clues: *I used to be a vegetarian, but I started having intense turkey cravings, so now I'm omnivorous.*

List three **omnivorous** animals.

dogs
cats
fish

Write a sentence using the word **omnivorous**.

unlike my sister, I am omnivorous

# *latent* (adj)

Context clues: *After just a few sessions with the psychiatrist, Andy's latent fears started to come to the surface.*

Underline the words that are not similar to **latent**.

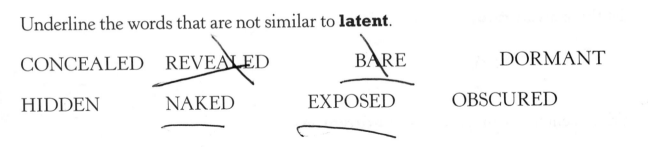

CONCEALED    REVEALED           BARE           DORMANT

HIDDEN       NAKED        EXPOSED        OBSCURED

Write a sentence using the word **latent**.

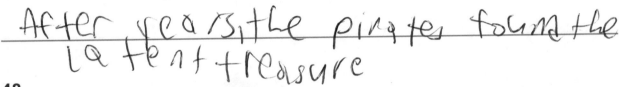

After years, the pirates found the latent treasure

# *quixotic* (adj)

Context clues: *When she turned eighteen, Lily set out on a quixotic pursuit of rollerskating fame.*

Underline the words that are synonymous with **quixotic**.

DREAMY     UNREALISTIC     PRAGMATIC     ROMANTIC

Write a sentence using the word **quixotic**.

Maytal has this qhixotic wish
tha 7 she will marry yehuda levin
her favorine singer

# *charlatan* (n)

Context clues: *Late-night TV is full of charlatans selling weight loss products and gas mileage improvers.*

Underline the words that describe a **charlatan**.

PHONY             SINCERE        FAKE        SPURIOUS

COUNTERFEIT     GENUINE      FRAUDULENT    BOGUS

Write a sentence using the word **charlatan**.

_____

# *tangible* (adj)

Context clues: *Brian went to the gym faithfully but, to his frustration, didn't see any tangible improvement in his physique.*

Circle the **tangible** items and cross out the **intangible** items.

JUSTICE        BRICK        GRASS        FREEDOM        AUTOMOBILE

DINNER         DESPAIR      BANANA       YELLOW         COMPUTER

Write a sentence using the word **tangible**.

_____

# *stagnant* (adj)

Context clues: *The stagnant pond attracts mosquitoes.*

Complete the words to create two synonyms of **stagnant**.

st i l l

dor m a n t

Write a sentence using the word **stagnant**.

Stay stagnant, I'll get your mother.

# *burgeon* (v)

Context clues: *After the fight was over, Mikey had a swollen lip and a burgeoning black eye.*

Complete the words to create two antonyms of **burgeon**.

Wi n_ _

Wa n e

Write a sentence using the word **burgeon**.

That rose is burgeon

# *deprecate* (v)

Context clues: *Sylvia deprecated her opponent in the strongest terms, calling her a cheat, a liar, and an incompetent buffoon.*

Have you **deprecated** anyone or anything recently? Explain.

Yes, My Mom, In the Shops I ga[...]
her dirty boots

Write a sentence using the word **deprecate**.

In politices, many people depre[...]
their opponent.

# *morose* (adj)

Context clues: *Edward, looking morose, stared out at the rain and felt sorry for himself.*

Underline the words that are not similar to **morose**.

GLUM          MISERABLE          <u>ELATED</u>          DEPRESSED

<u>EUPHORIC</u>          BLUE          ECSTATIC          <u>JUBILANT</u>

Write a sentence using the word **morose**.

Perri was very morose that she didn't get to go to school that day.

# *arduous* (adj)

Context clues: *Nellie was assigned the arduous task of cleaning the floor with a toothbrush.*

Complete the words to create two synonyms of **arduous**.

gru __l__ __l__ ing

labor __i__ __o__ u s

Write a sentence using the word **arduous**.

People in the great Dipression went throcgu ardous times

# *astute* (adj)

Context clues: *With remarkable astuteness, Sherlock identified his visitor as an editor.*

Underline the words that describe characteristics of an **astute** person.

WISE            JUDICIOUS            GULLIBLE        OBSERVANT

Write a sentence using the word **astute**.

The tarate teacher was a very astute man

**57**

# *superficial* (adj)

Context clues: *Everyone assumes that Ramona is superficial, because she only dates male models.*

Complete the words to create two antonyms of **superficial**.

int _ _ n _ _

pr _ _ _ _ n _

Write a sentence using the word **superficial**.

_____

# *nonchalant* (adj)

Context clues: *Greg's Bermuda shorts, Hawaiian shirt, and flip-flops perfectly match his nonchalant attitude.*

List five things about which you have a **nonchalant** attitude.

clothes          who my favorite teacher is
taste in things
the way I act in school
who I'm friends with

Write a sentence using the word **nonchalant**.

Sophie is a very nonchalant person, she doesn't
care what people think about her personality
and clothes.

# *catharsis* (n)

Context clues: *Everyone sobbed at the end of the play and then felt better after the cathartic experience.*

Underline the verbs that might be associated with **catharsis**.

LAUGH          SMELL          WEEP          BALANCE          YELL

Write a sentence using the word **catharsis**.

_____

# *prodigious* (adj)

Context clues: *The young novelist, who had prodigious talent, won the Pulitzer Prize when she was in her mid-twenties.*

Circle the words that are synonyms for **prodigious** and cross out the words that are not synonyms for **prodigious**.

IMPRESSIVE  PHENOMENAL  AVERAGE  NORMAL

TYPICAL  COMMON  UNUSUAL  MUNDANE

Write a sentence using the word **prodigious**.

Ali has a prodigious talent of piano. He can look at a piece and play it, and ca compose music easily.

# *nullify* (v)

Context clues: *The impressive test results were nullified when it was discovered that the entire class had cheated.*

Complete the words to create two synonyms of **nullify**.

neg <u>a t e</u>

abol <u>i s h</u>

Write a sentence using the word **nullify**.

The electon was nullify when they found out 500 people voted trice.

# *zealot* (n)

Context clues: *The crazed zealot paraded through the street waving a sign that read "The End is Near."*

Write a sentence using the word **zealot**.

They could name the Philly Phanatic the Philly Zealot.

# *ostensible* (adj)

Context clues: *Pete's ostensible reason for joining SADD was to combat drunk driving, but he really joined to impress college admissions officials.*

Complete the words to create two synonyms of **ostensible**.

supp os e d

perc e i ve d

Write a sentence using the word **ostensible**.

"Does th's dress make me

# *hyperbole* (n)

Context clues: *Polly, who is often guilty of hyperbole, claimed she'd caught a fish the size of a Buick.*

Write a few sentences using **hyperboles** about your school cafeteria.

My School Cafeteria's food

# *requisite* (n)

Context clues: *If you want to be popular, name-brand clothes are requisite.*

List five **requisites** for one of the following: graduating from high school, becoming President of the United States, playing professional sports.

President!
oVer 32
Born in U.S.A

Smart
Confident

Commited

Write a sentence using the word **requisite**.

In gim, it is requisite to wear your
gim clothes.

# *genre* (n)

Context clues: *Conventional wisdom says that women's favorite film genre is romantic comedy, but many women prefer action or suspense.*

Write a sentence or two about your favorite movie **genre** and your favorite literature **genre**. I really like comedy because I love to laugh.

# *convergence* (n)

Context clues: *Estefan and Chris were an unbeatable team. Together, they symbolized the convergence of brain and brawn.*

Complete the words to create two synonyms of **convergence**.

un _ _ n

jun _ _ _ _ _

Write a sentence using the word **convergence**.

*The converge of the story is never given*

# *intrepid* (adj)

Context clues: *The intrepid astronauts braved the unexplored planet.*

List five professions that require **intrepidness**.

Doctor President Bodygaurd
Explorer
Astronauts

Write a sentence using the word **intrepid**.

Her intrepid quality got her through the American Idol audition and into the next round

# *ostentatious* (adj)

Context clues: *The gangster's ostentatious mansion was full of marble fountains, platinum faucets, and oriental rugs.*

Write a few sentences about someone you know who is **ostentatious**.

Write a sentence using the word **ostentatious**.

# *anomaly* (n)

Context clues: *As a smart, nice girl who wasn't interested in popularity, Bindu was a total anomaly in her school.*

Complete the words to create two synonyms of **anomaly**.

ir e g u l a r i t y

varia _ _ _

Write a sentence using the word **anomaly**.

_____

# *endemic* (adj)

Context clues: *Although celebrities are endemic to L.A., Lee didn't see any when he visited.*

List five things that are **endemic** to your high school.

ATM
GOSSiP
TV
Sports
cellphones

Write a sentence using the word **endemic**.

In hospitals, doctors and
nurses are endemic.

# *relegate* (v)

*[handwritten: Being sent down]*

Context clues: *After arguing with a customer, Catie was barred from waiting on tables and relegated to the kitchen.*

Cross out the words that are not synonyms of **relegate**.

PROMOTE *[crossed out]*      DOWNGRADE      DEMOTE      DEVALUE

ELEVATE *[crossed out]*      ADVANCE *[crossed out]*      DIMINISH      LESSEN

Write a sentence using the word **relegate**.

*[handwritten: As she got tired, her attension span seared to relegate.]*

73

# *cursory* (adj)

Context clues: *Matt took a cursory look at the newspaper headlines as he stood at the counter eating his granola.*

Complete the words to create two antonyms of **cursory**.

thor o u g h

method i c a l

Write a sentence using the word **cursory**.

I take a cursory look at the sports page

# *callous* (adj) ~ *hard*

Context clues: *With a callous laugh, Melissa turned her back on her sobbing lover and walked off with the oil tycoon.*

*rich person / Donald Duck*

Underline the words that are synonymous with **callous**.

UNFEELING          TENDER          HEARTLESS          SYMPATHETIC

EMPATHETIC          KINDLY          CRASS          UNSYMPATHETIC

Write a sentence using the word **callous**.

She gave a callous smirk to her classmate who walked away happy she was the only one who got an A.

© 2004 SparkNotes LLC

# *antagonist* (n)

Context clues: *Whenever the antagonist came onstage, the little kids in the audience hissed and booed.*

Complete the words to create two synonyms of **antagonist**.

r i v a l

en e m y

Write a sentence using the word **antagonist**.

Every baseball team's antagonist
is the umpires.

# *temerity* (n)

Context clues: *Even though she didn't study for the test at all, Endeara had the temerity to insist that she deserved an A on it.*

Underline the words that are synonymous with **temerity**.

BOLD    RASH    TIMID    IMPUDENT    COY

Write a sentence using the word **temerity**.

The guy at the foot ball
game had the temerity to
stole up the whole game

77

# *hackneyed* (adj) *corny*

Context clues: *Max always uses that hackneyed old pickup line, "Is your father a thief? Because someone stole the stars and put them in your eyes."*

Cross out the words that are not synonyms of **hackneyed**.

CLICHÉ          TRITE          SIGNIFICANT          IMAGINATIVE

Write a sentence using the word **hackneyed**.

"Have you done all your homework" is one of my parents' hackneyed questions.

*Volume → a lot of something*

# *voluminous* (adj)

Context clues: *Bernardo's voluminous writing included everything from love poetry to journal entries to news articles.*

Complete the words to create two synonyms of **voluminous**.

la**rge**

hu**ge**

Write a sentence using the word **voluminous**.

I have a voluminous amount of home. work.

© 2004 SparkNotes LLC

# *lope* (v)

Context clues: *Collins loped toward the soccer field, carrying his bag and kicking the ball.*

Underline the words that are synonyms of **lope**.

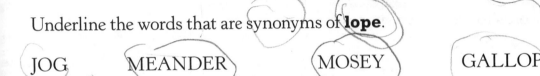

JOG          MEANDER          MOSEY          GALLOP

Write a sentence using the word **lope**.

She loped to school because
she went to bed at 12 and woke up
at 6.

# *undulate* (v)

Context clues: *The belly dancer undulated toward her captive audience.*

Complete the words to create two synonyms of **undulate**.

r o l l

r i pp l e

Write a sentence using the word **undulate**.

Let's undulate doln the hill.

# supercilious (adj)

_superior_ _King_ _Queen_ ?

_opposite_ _poor_

Context clues: _With a supercilious sniff, Marie kicked the peasants out of the way and swept into her carriage._

Complete the words to create two antonyms of **supercilious**.

hum b l e

m e e k

Write a sentence using the word **supercilious**.

_____

# *infamy* (n)

Franklin Delano Roosvelt FDR
* This is a day that will live in infamy. Dec. 7, 1941

Context clues: *In fourth grade circles, Mikey was infamous for his cruel bullying techniques.*

List five people you consider **infamous**.

Asa Ra Benladin Hitler Saddam Hussein
Brithey Spears Terrel owens

Write a sentence using the word **infamy.**

ASama Benladin is in famous for doing bad things to Amera!

# *esoteric* (adj)

Context clues: *According to Delia's esoteric religious beliefs, good people go to a city like Manhattan when they die.*

Cross out the words that are not synonyms of **esoteric**.

ARCANE    ~~COMMON~~    OBSCURE    ~~STRAIGHTFORWARD~~

CRYPTIC    ABSTRUSE    ~~HUMOROUS~~    ~~SIMPLE~~

Write a sentence using the word **esoteric**.

Amanda has a very esoteric theory, it's that birds+fish = Humans

# imminent (adj)

*[handwritten: happen any time]*  *[handwritten: eminent – high regard]*

---

Context clues: *To prepare for the imminent storm, Brian purchased snow boots and a shovel.*

List five **imminent** events in your life.

*[handwritten:]*
Sleep    Komputer
school    shower
breakfast

Write a sentence using the word **imminent**.

*[handwritten:]* My mom rememded me to study for the imminent test.

# clemency (n)

*citation*

Context clues: *Judge Leda granted clemency to the criminal, citing the criminal's difficult childhood and sincere repentance for his crimes.*

Cross out the words that are not synonymous with **clemency**.

VENGEANCE　　FORGIVENESS　　COMPASSION　　ANGER

HARSHNESS　　LENIENCY　　RETRIBUTION　　PITY

*revenge*

Write a sentence using the word **clemency**.

_____

# *amicable* (adj) ~ friendly

Context clues: *Despite the constant bickering that had characterized their marriage, their divorce was more amicable than most.*

Complete the words to create two antonyms of **amicable**.

Con**ten**tious → contender

**dis**agreeable

Write a sentence using the word **amicable**.

_____

# *anachronism* (n)

Context clues: *The author included an interesting anachronism in his novel: hanging above the fireplace in the knight's castle was a flat screen TV.*

List five things that would be **anachronisms** in a novel or movie about ancient Egypt.

*out of place*

*cell Phone    iPod*
*   CP      dishwasher*
*   TV*

Write a sentence using the word **anachronism**.

*On the airplane, I was doing an achronism.*

# *prodigal* (adj)

Context clues: *In the parable, the prodigal son lives a lavish lifestyle before repenting and returning to his father.*

Complete the words to create two synonyms of **prodigal**.

ext _a_ _gant

was _e_f_l

Write a sentence using the word **prodigal**.

All of the prodigal kids went to Las vegas after graduation.

# *vindicate* (v)

*[handwritten: Someone who "rats" on you]*

Context clues: *After the secret files were made public, the informant was completely vindicated.*

*[handwritten: innocent]*

Underline the words that might be associated with a **vindicated** person.

INNOCENCE          DEFEND          CLAIM          DELAY

ASSERT          DEFINE          COMPREHEND          ENJOY

Write a sentence using the word **vindicate**.

*[handwritten: The judge decided he was vindicated.]*

# *formidable* (adj) *indestructible*

Context clues: *With her surprising strength and her mastery of karate, Lizzy made a formidable opponent.*

List five emotions you might feel when confronted with something **formidable**.

*afraid → scared – nervous*
*surprised*

Write a sentence using the word **formidable**.

*Superman's formidable.*

# *meander* (v)

Context clues: *The young couple meandered through the amusement park, stopping at whatever rides looked appealing.*

Complete the words to create two synonyms of **meander**.

ra _ _ _ e

r _ v _

Write a sentence using the word **meander**.

_____

# *dubious* (adj)

Context clues: *The trapeze instructor told Medina she could do it, but Medina looked dubious and refused to step off the platform.*

Complete the words to create two antonyms of **dubious**.

cer _ _ _ _

s _ _ e

Write a sentence using the word **dubious**.

# *prescient* (adj)

Context clues: *The fortuneteller at the carnival was either prescient or extremely lucky when she predicted that I would win the lottery; I just sent her a check for $1,000 from my winnings.*

List five things about which you wish you could be **prescient**.

Write a sentence using the word **prescient**.

*VOCABULARY*

© 2004 SparkNotes LLC

# *debacle* (n)

Context clues: *The wedding turned into a complete debacle; not only did the bride and groom get into a screaming match at the reception, but the band never showed up and the cake was inedible.*

Underline the words that are synonyms of **debacle**.

CALAMITY     CATASTROPHE            EPIPHANY   FIASCO

OBSTACLE     EVENT            TRAGEDY            AFFAIR

Write a sentence using the word **debacle**.

# *gesticulate* (v)

Context clues: *I couldn't hear them, but it was clear from their angry gesticulations that they were having an argument.*

List a few ways you **gesticulate** when you speak.

Write a sentence using the word **gesticulate**.

# *vestige* (n)

Context clues: *Josh held on to a few vestiges of his relationship with Lee, including a dried rose and a faded polaroid.*

Complete the words to create two synonyms of **vestige**.

rem _ _ _ s

t _ _ _ e

Write a sentence using the word **vestige**.

# *ogle* (v)

Context clues: *When the buff movie star came to town to shoot his new film, all the girls skipped school to ogle him.*

List five things that might cause people to **ogle**.

Write a sentence using the word **ogle**.

# *relic* (n)

Context clues: *Millions of people journeyed to the church to worship the relic of Saint James.*

Underline the words that could be associated with **relic**.

TRENDY     SACRED     ANCIENT     TRIVIAL

RELIGIOUS     OLD     HISTORICAL     VENERATED

Write a sentence using the word **relic**.

_____

# *arbiter* (n)

Context clues: *The company called in a professional arbiter to help the warring vice presidents work out their problems.*

Have you ever had a fight or a disagreement that might have benefited from an **arbiter**'s advice? Explain.

Write a sentence using the word **arbiter**.

# *stoic* (adj)

Context clues: *Zeke was stoic in the face of the terrible heat and the vast desert, even though he was lost and had almost no water left.*

Complete the words to create two synonyms of **stoic**.

a _ _ the _ _ c

_ _ emo _ _ _ _ al

Write a sentence using the word **stoic**.

*...ns persuaded the city council to rescind the ban on chewing*

Complete the words to create two synonyms of **rescind**.

can _ _ _

un _ _

Write a sentence using the word **rescind**.

_____

# *maverick* (n)

Context clues: *The maverick cop often caught criminals, but his refusal to listen to his superiors meant that he was never promoted.*

Write a sentence using the word **maverick**.

# *ocution* (n)

*: Justin couldn't remember the answer, so he resorted to circumlocution,* *ma... ...assionate but irrelevant speech about Lincoln's childhood.*

Write a short dialogue between two people in which one uses **circumlocution** to hide his or her ignorance.

Write a sentence using the word **circumlocution**.

# *vapid* (adj)

Context clues: *The vapid sorority sister had nothing to talk about besides clothes and parties.*

Complete the words to create two synonyms of **vapid**.

b _ _ _ d

insip _ _

Write a sentence using the word **vapid**.

_____

# *demagogue* (n)

Context clues: *As the demagogue finished his emotional speech, the masses cheered wildly in the plaza.*

Underline the words that describe characteristics of a **demagogue**.

HUMBLE          CHARISMATIC          PASSIONATE          TIMID

MEEK            TIMOROUS             COMPELLING

Write a sentence using the word **demagogue**.

_____

# *admonish* (v)

Context clues: *Betty gently admonished her new puppy for yipping when a stranger came to the door.*

Complete the words to create two synonyms of **admonish**.

re _ _ k _

re _ _ _ v _

Write a sentence using the word **admonish**.

_____

# *placid* (adj)

Context clues: *Mike, who had hoped to go surfing, cursed the unusually placid water.*

List five synonyms of **placid**.

Write a sentence using the word **placid**.

# *cumbersome* (adj)

Context clues: *It took them two hours to get the cumbersome package up the stairs.*

Underline the words that are synonyms of **cumbersome**.

MANAGEABLE    UNWIELDY    BULKY    COMPACT

WEIGHTY    ONEROUS    CONTROLLABLE    UNGAINLY

Write a sentence using the word **cumbersome**.

# *unscathed* (adj)

Context clues: *He had a couple of close calls, but he ended up making it out of the battle unscathed.*

Complete the words to create two synonyms of **unscathed**.

un _ _ _ _

un _ _ _ _ ed

Write a sentence using the word **unscathed**.

_____

# *tedious* (adj)

Context clues: *Everyone assumed the speaker would be fascinating, but he turned out to be so tedious that half the audience fell asleep.*

List five activities you find **tedious**.

Write a sentence using the word **tedious**.

# *skeptic* (n)

Context clues: *The preacher promised that sinners would be punished in the afterlife, but some skeptics in the audience seemed unconvinced.*

Underline the words that describe characteristics of a **skeptic**.

ACCEPTANCE    DISBELIEF    OPTIMISM    PESSIMISM

CYNICISM    APPROVAL    OPENNESS    DISTRUST

Write a sentence using the word **skeptic**.

_____

# *altruism* (n)

Context clues: *Mrs. Lew's donation was entirely altruistic; she insisted on remaining anonymous.*

Name a few acts of **altruism** you have witnessed or read about recently.

Write a sentence using the word **altruism**.

# *subtle* (adj)

Context clues: *With just a subtle motion of her head, Gloria managed to communicate to her friends that they should run away.*

Complete the words to create two antonyms of **subtle**.

notice _ _ _ _

overs _ _ t _ _

Write a sentence using the word **subtle**.

_____

# *thrifty* (adj)

Context clues: *Christian, who is renowned for his thriftiness, mends his socks and reuses his lunch bags in order to save money.*

Underline the words that might be associated with **thrifty**.

PRODIGAL     SPENDTHRIFT     MISER     PENNY-PINCHING

WASTEFUL     STINGY     EXTRAVAGANT     CONSERVATIVE

Write a sentence using the word **thrifty**.

_____

# *antithesis* (n)

Context clues: *With his brains and interest in classical music, Lou is the antithesis of the stereotypical jock.*

Write the **antithesis** of each word.

GOOD _____     PEACE _____

NIGHT _____     COLD _____

HAPPY _____     SICK _____

Write a sentence using the word **antithesis**.

# *hindrance* (n)

Context clues: *Little Lucy thought she was helping her mother in the kitchen, but her efforts were actually more of a hindrance than a help.*

Complete the words to create two synonyms of **hindrance**.

barr _ _ _

ob _ _ ruc _ _ _ _

Write a sentence using the word **hindrance**.

_____

# *brevity* (n)

Context clues: *Thanks to the brevity of the speaker's remarks, the assembly was over in about ten minutes.*

Cross out the words that are not synonymous with **brevity**.

BRIEF                CONCISE          PROLIFIC          VERBOSE

TERSE                SUCCINCT         LENGTHY           EXTENSIVE

Write a sentence using the word **brevity**.

_____

# *plethora* (n)

Context clues: *Jason was so overwhelmed by the plethora of items at the salad bar that he couldn't decide what to get.*

Complete the words to create two antonyms of **plethora**.

scar _ _ _ _

d _ f _ c _ t

Write a sentence using the word **plethora**.

_____

# *nostalgic* (adj)

Context clues: *After stumbling across a box of her old stuffed animals, Margaret felt nostalgic for her childhood.*

List five things from your childhood about which you are **nostalgic**.

Write a sentence using the word **nostalgic**.

# *conundrum* (n)

Context clues: *Faced with the conundrum of how to break up with his girlfriend without hurting her feelings, Pete turned to his mother for advice.*

Complete the words to create two synonyms of **conundrum**.

e _ _ g _ _

pr _ _ _ _ _

Write a sentence using the word **conundrum**.

_____

# *proselytize* (v)

Context clues: *When the Jehovah's Witnesses come to proselytize, Ms. Lott tells them she's a devil worshipper.*

Underline the words that might be associated with **proselytize**.

DISCIPLE      FOREIGNER      DISCOVER      PROPHET

PREACH      CONVERT      DIGRESS      DELAY

Write a sentence using the word **proselytize**.

# *erudite* (adj)

Context clues: *The erudite professor impressed students with her deep knowledge.*

Complete the words to create two antonyms of **erudite**.

un _ d _ c _ _ _ d

ig _ _ _ _ _ _

Write a sentence using the word **erudite**.

# *accolade* (n)

Context clues: *Ms. Frank has received accolades for her support of the arts and her campaigns for human rights.*

List **accolades** you would like to earn or win.

Write a sentence using the word **accolade**.

# *bellicose* (adj)

Context clues: *The bellicose general was itching to send his troops into battle.*

List five antonyms of **bellicose**.

Write a sentence using the word **bellicose**.

# *duplicity* (n)

Context clues: *Pierre was shocked by the duplicity of his girlfriend, who for a year had been hiding her career as a circus performer.*

Cross out the words that are not associated with **duplicity**.

PATRIOT            TRUTH            DECEIT            HONOR

DECEPTION          REALITY          TRICKERY         FRAUD

Write a sentence using the word **duplicity**.

_____

# *unkempt* (adj)

Context clues: *After sleeping on the beach for two nights in a row, Francine had smelly clothes and unkempt hair.*

Complete the words to create two synonyms of **unkempt**.

m _ _ _ y

un _ _ dy

Write a sentence using the word **unkempt**.

_____

# *premonition* (n)

Context clues: *Just before lightning struck, Emile had a premonition that something terrible was going to happen to the guy standing in the middle of the golf course.*

Underline the words that are synonymous with **premonition**.

OMEN                    RELIC          INTUITION        HUNCH

AFTERTHOUGHT       FEELING        REMINDER        MEMENTO

Write a sentence using the word **premonition**.

_____

VOCABULARY

© 2004 SparkNotes LLC

# *construe* (v)

Context clues: *From what the detective could construe, jealousy caused the crime.*

Complete the words to create two synonyms of **construe**.

inter _ _ e _

i _ f _ r

Write a sentence using the word **construe**.

_____

# *delve* (v)

Context clues: *After meeting the dashing and handsome Manuel, Steph delved into her studies of Spanish with real enthusiasm.*

Cross out the words that are not synonyms of **delve**.

EXAMINE          CLIMB                INVESTIGATE

PROBE            COMPOUND             EXPLORE          INQUIRE

Write a sentence using the word **delve**.

# *pariah* (n)

Context clues: *Sam's constant tattling and brownnosing made him a pariah at school.*

Underline the words that might be associated with **pariah**.

ACCEPTANCE          DIFFERENT          SHUN          INSIDER

CONFORM          OUTSIDER          EXILE          BELONG

Write a sentence using the word **pariah**.

_____

# *contort* (v)

Context clues: *As the audience gasped, Marvelo contorted himself until he was the size of a shoebox.*

List five things that one could **contort**.

Write a sentence using the word **contort**.

# *tantalize* (v)

Context clues: *After weeks of dieting, Val found freshly baked bread almost painfully tantalizing.*

Write a sentence using the word **tantalize**.

# *phobia* (n)

Context clues: *Years of therapy helped Mark overcome his many phobias, including his intense fear of bananas.*

List five **phobias** you've heard of.

Write a sentence using the word **phobia**.

# *antipathy* (n)

Context clues: *Kerrie felt such intense antipathy toward Mr. Gibbons that she involuntarily growled whenever she saw him.*

Complete the words to create two antonyms of **antipathy**.

app _ _ v _ l

l _ _ e

Write a sentence using the word **antipathy**.

# *extol* (v)

Context clues: *Over dinner, the vice president extolled the virtues of his new dog, Cookie.*

Write a sentence using the word **extol**.

# *resolute* (adj)

Context clues: *Paul was resolute in his desire to win the pie-eating contest.*

Underline the words that are synonymous with **resolute**.

WISHY-WASHY  FIRM  UNBENDING  RESOLVED

UNDECIDED  STUBBORN  UNWAVERING  STEADFAST

Write a sentence using the word **resolute**.

# *proximity* (n)

Context clues: *The houses are in such close proximity that when Mrs. Shah sneezes, Mrs. Jennings says, "Bless you."*

Complete the words to create two synonyms of **proximity**.

v _ c _ _ _ t _

cl _ s _ n _ _ _

Write a sentence using the word **proximity**.

# *inconsequential* (adj)

Context clues: *The designer pays attention to every detail, even seemingly inconsequential ones like the width of buttonholes.*

Complete the words to create two antonyms of **inconsequential**.

imp _ _ _ _ _ _

si _ _ _ f _ _ _ _ t

Write a sentence using the word **inconsequential**.

_____

# *cogent* (adj)

Context clues: *Sylvester made such a cogent argument in favor of gun control that his debating opponent was left speechless.*

Cross out the words that are not synonyms of **cogent**.

CONVINCING     ILLOGICAL     INCOHERENT     SOUND

REASONABLE     PERSUASIVE     AMBIGUOUS     OBTUSE

Write a sentence using the word **cogent**.

_____

# *desultory* (adj)

Context clues: *Rose cleaned her room in a desultory fashion, folding shirts for a few minutes, staring out the window for a while, and then moving some pens from one drawer to another.*

Complete the words to create two antonyms of **desultory**.

f _ c _ s _ _

me _ _ _ d _ ca _

Write a sentence using the word **desultory**.

# *platitude* (n)

Context clues: *After Madison's mother died, the last thing she wanted to hear was platitudes like "She's in a better place."*

Underline the words that describe a **platitude**.

CLICHÉ          INSIPID        BANAL          INTREPID

INSIGHTFUL      TRITE          THOUGHTFUL     DEEP

Write a sentence using the word **platitude**.

# *static* (adj)

Context clues: *The community, once constantly in flux, has become static in recent years.*

Complete the words to create two synonyms of **static**.

st _ _ _ _ _ ary

m _ _ _ _ _ l _ ss

Write a sentence using the word **static**.

_____

# *flagrant* (adj)

Context clues: *Carson's flagrant disregard for his wife's feelings led to a bitter, expensive divorce.*

Underline the synonyms of **flagrant** and cross out the antonyms of **flagrant**.

OVERT          HIDDEN          BLATANT          STEALTHY

BRAZEN          COVERT          OBVIOUS          DELIBERATE

Write a sentence using the word **flagrant**.

_____

# *accouterments* (n)

Context clues: *The bag was stuffed with sunscreen, cheap novels, towels, and other accouterments of a day at the beach.*

Make a list five **accouterments** that you would need for a road trip.

Write a sentence using the word **accouterments**.

# *stymie* (v)

Context clues: *Brian worked on the crossword for almost four hours, but he was stymied by nineteen across and eventually gave up in disgust.*

Complete the words to create two synonyms of **stymie**.

b _ wil _ _ _

_ aff_ _

Write a sentence using the word **stymie**.

_____

# *luminous* (adj)

Context clues: *The flight attendant captivated passengers with her melodious voice and luminous smile.*

List five things that could be described as **luminous**.

Write a sentence using the word **luminous**.

# *hiatus* (n)

Context clues: *"I think we need a hiatus from this relationship,"* said Melody. *"You're driving me crazy, and I want to try dating other people for a while."*

If you could take a **hiatus** from school, where would you go, and what would you do there?

Write a sentence using the word **hiatus**.

_____

**148**

# *remuneration* (n)

Context clues: *No remuneration would truly compensate substitute teachers for the nightmares they go through every day.*

Cross out the words that are not associated with **remuneration**.

REWARD          WINNINGS          SALARY          JACKPOT

WAGES          EARNINGS          RECOMPENSE          LOTTERY

Write a sentence using the word **remuneration**.

_____

# *grovel* (v)

Context clues: *I refuse to grovel. On second thought, can I please, please, please borrow your car?*

Write a short dialogue between two people in which one person **grovels** to the other.

Write a sentence using the word **grovel**.

# *compendium* (n)

Context clues: *When Hannah gets sick, she likes to curl up with a bowl of chicken soup and her favorite compendium of mystery stories.*

Cross out the words that are not associated with **compendium**.

VERBOSE          SYNOPSIS          VOLUMINOUS          LENGTHY

ABSTRACT          RAMBLING          DIGEST          EXTENSIVE

Write a sentence using the word **compendium**.

_____

# *redoubtable* (adj)

Context clues: *Theo had such redoubtable knowledge of* The Simpsons *that he was asked to fact-check a book about the show.*

Complete the words to create two synonyms of **redoubtable**.

fo _ _ _ _ _ _ le

f _ _ r _ ome

Write a sentence using the word **redoubtable**.

_____

# *incantation* (n)

Context clues: *The witch murmured an incantation as she added green liquid to the pot.*

Write an **incantation** of your own.

# *embellish* (v)

Context clues: *Claudia embellished her story; she claimed that not only had a modeling company offered her a contract, but an agent had told her she should be an actress.*

Rewrite this sentence, **embellishing** it: *The cat climbed up the tree, and the fireman rescued it.*

Write a sentence using the word **embellish**.

© 2004 SparkNotes LLC

# *obstreperous* (adj)

Context clues: *The obstreperous mule came to a halt in the middle of the canyon and refused to walk another step.*

Complete the words to create two antonyms of **obstreperous**.

su _ _ _ ss _ _ e

y _ _ _ ding

Write a sentence using the word **obstreperous**.

# *vicarious* (adj)

Context clues: *After watching Brady throw a touchdown pass, Drew felt a vicarious thrill of excitement.*

Describe the **vicarious** pleasure you take in something—the riches of celebrities, the accomplishments of people you know, etc.

Write a sentence using the word **vicarious**.

# *parsimonious* (adj)

Context clues: *Everyone calls the lunch lady "Parsimonious Patty" because she refuses to give out more than ten french fries per serving.*

Underline the words that are synonyms of **parsimonious**.

PHILANTHROPIC    MISERLY    THRIFTY    GENEROUS

GIVING    FRUGAL    LIBERAL    BOUNTIFUL

Write a sentence using the word **parsimonious**.

_____

# *embroil* (v)

Context clues: *Manny and James found themselves embroiled in a heated argument about who had eaten more tacos.*

Complete the words to create two synonyms of **embroil**.

en _ _ ng _ _

_ _ _ _ _ twine

Write a sentence using the word **embroil**.

_____

# *paradigm* (n)

Context clues: *Ms. Lynn's is a paradigm of successful AP instruction.*

Cross out the words that are not synonyms of **paradigm**.

ARCHETYPE     TYPOGRAPHY     EXAMPLE     INDICATION

PROTOTYPE     DEVIATION     STANDARD     PARAGRAPH

Write a sentence using the word **paradigm**.

_____

# *aphorism* (n)

Context clues: *Charlie's bankruptcy proves the truth of that old aphorism: "A fool and his money are soon parted."*

Write two **aphorisms** of your own about any two of the following topics: school, love, luck, wisdom, success, hard work.

Write a sentence using the word **aphorism**.

# *herald* (n)

Context clues: *The herald dashed into the court, stopped to catch his breath, and said, "I bring great news!"*

Complete the words to create two synonyms of **herald**.

m _ _ _ _ _ ger

har_ _ _ ger

Write a sentence using the word **herald**.

_____

# *bulwark* (n)

Context clues: *The gate proved to be an insufficient bulwark against the rampaging crowds.*

Cross out the words that are not synonyms of **bulwark**.

EMBANKMENT          PASSAGEWAY          RAMPART          ROOM

SLALOM          BARRICADE          SAFEGUARD          HOUSE

Write a sentence using the word **bulwark**.

# *ineluctable* (adj)

Context clues: *There was no ignoring the ineluctable fact that after graduation, everyone without a trust fund had to either go to college or find a job.*

Complete the words to create two antonyms of **ineluctable**.

a _ _ i _ _ _ l _

pre_ _ _ _ _ _ _

Write a sentence using the word **ineluctable**.

# *repartee* (n)

Context clues: *Compared to the witty repartee that fills Oscar Wilde's plays, everyday conversation is banal and slow.*

Write a short **repartee** between two characters. Use screenplay or play form.

# *fidelity* (n)

Context clues: *Irene swore everlasting fidelity to Yuri, but the very next weekend, she kissed another guy at a party.*

Cross out the words that are not synonyms of **fidelity**.

FAITHFULNESS   TREACHERY   UNCONFORMITY   DEVOTION

DEVIANCE   DEPENDABILITY   WASTEFULNESS   RELIABILITY

Write a sentence using the word **fidelity**.

_____

# *baroque* (adj)

Context clues: *The baroque argument was full of flourishes and ornaments.*

Complete the words to create two antonyms of **baroque**.

s _ _ ple

s _ _ _ k

# *voracious* and *veracious* (adj)

Context clues: *Stuart has a voracious appetite and can eat an entire box of cereal in one sitting, but at least he's veracious about it.*

Fill in the blanks with either **voracious** or **veracious**.

Tessa, who has a _____ interest in worms, spends every free minute digging in the dirt.

No one is more _____ than Joe; he founded the Honor Society.

_____

# *bizarre* and *bazaar* (n)

Context clues: *We found the most bizarre cufflinks at the bazaar.*

Fill in the blanks with either **bizarre** or **bazaar**.

Every weekend he peddles his wares at the _____ on the other side of town.

His behavior is so _____ that everyone calls him Weird Walter.

# *illusion* and *allusion* (n)

Context clues: *I didn't get a single one of his allusions, but I managed to create the illusion that I did.*

Fill in the blanks with either **illusion** or **allusion**.

*Did you catch my learned* _____ *to Shakespeare?*

*The kids were entirely fooled by the magician's* _____.

# *continual* and *continuous* (adj)

Context clues: *The continual wailing of the car alarm infuriated Matt and prevented him from getting eight hours of continuous sleep.*

Fill in the blanks with either **continual** or **continuous**.

The _____ whine of the toddler got on my last nerve.

The _____ playback feature on my MP3 player allows me to listen as long as I like.

# *amoral* and *immoral* (adj)

Context clues: *Despite his immoral behavior, the criminal was not entirely amoral.*

Fill in the blanks with either **amoral** or **immoral**.

*Unless he can prove he understands the difference between right and wrong, I'll have to conclude that he is completely _____.*

*The _____ behavior of that businessman comes as no surprise to me.*

# *prosecute* and *persecute* (v)

Context clues: *Because the anti-fur activist violently persecuted women with fur coats, the attorney decided to prosecute her.*

Fill in the blanks with either **prosecuted** or **persecuted**.

*The case was expertly _____ by Ms. Flockhart.*

*Many people who are _____ in high school grow up to be rich and successful.*

# *complement* and *compliment* (v)

Context clues: *Her fuzzy pink hat and gloves, which complement each other, always win many compliments.*

Fill in the blanks with either **complement** or **compliment**.

*Olive and Popeye _____ each other well; they make a nice couple.*

*To win her heart, simply _____ her shoes.*

# *predominate* and *predominant* (adj)

Context clues: *Ruthlessness, his predominant characteristic, was what allowed him to predominate the french fry industry.*

Fill in the blanks with either **predominate** or **predominant**.

*If she manages to _____, she'll win a million dollars.*

*The_____ feature of her face was her large green eyes.*

# *discreet* and *discrete* (adj)

Context clues: *If we break into discrete groups, we can gossip more discreetly.*

Fill in the blanks with either **discreet** or **discrete**.

The smoking policy doesn't cover teachers; we need a _____ policy for them.

Please be _____; I don't want the whole school knowing what I did.

# *material* and *materiel* (n)

Context clues: *The reporter stumbled across some great material for her article when she discovered that the military was using illegal materiel.*

Fill in the blanks with either **material** or **materiel**.

*To make some money, the army has started selling _____ to civilians.*

*This _____ feels like velvet.*

# *affect* (v) and *effect* (n)

Context clues: *Suzy hoped her lecture would affect the kids she was babysitting, but it had no effect at all: they continued pelting each other with water balloons.*

Fill in the blanks with either **affect** or **effect**.

*If you want to _____ the outcome of the election, you have to quit your job and join the campaign.*

*The unintended _____ of Opie's loud, off-key singing was to make the dogs outside start howling.*

# *imply* and *infer* (v)

Context clues: *From your furious tone of voice, I infer that you've found out about my criminal history; are you implying you don't want to date me anymore?*

Fill in the blanks with either **imply** or **infer**.

*Several telling details made it easy to _____ that the novel was really a thinly disguised account of the writer's own life.*

*Nick cried, "How dare you _____ that I killed the goldfish?"*

# *cite* (v) and *site* (n)

Context clues: *When researching your paper on ancient burial sites, take careful notes so you can cite your sources later.*

Fill in the blanks with either **cite** or **site**.

*The reporter made many fascinating claims, but failed to _____ his sources.*

*When they arrived at the _____, they found the photographer in tears and the model hiding in her trailer.*

# *principal* and *principle* (n)

Context clues: *"This summer," said the principal, "I hope you will continue to abide by the principles we have tried to instill in you during the school year."*

Fill in the blanks with either **principal** or **principle**.

*Yolanda is a woman of _____ who never follows the crowd.*

*We can only hope the new _____ isn't as mean and unfair as the old one.*

# Answers

1. **evanescent (adj):** fleeting, momentary, short-lived
*brief, temporary*

2. **negligible (adj):** of little importance; hardly noticeable
*TINY    NEGLIGIBLE    <u>MAJOR</u>    INSIGNIFICANT*

3. **capitulate (v):** to give up, to surrender
Answers will vary but may include *surrender* or *give up.*
Answers will vary but may include *resist* or *fight.*

4. **incessant (adj):** without end, persistent
*continuous, nonstop*

5. **utopia (n):** an ideal place, paradise
Answers will vary.

6. **lethargy (n):** laziness, tiredness, indolence
*energy, enthusiasm*

7. **fluctuate (v):** to change, to ebb and flow, to rise and fall

Answers will vary.

8. **capricious (adj):** variable, unpredictable, changeable

*erratic, whimsical*

9. **venerate (v):** to revere, to honor

*WORSHIP*          *LIONIZE*        *ESTEEM*        ~~*DISGRACE*~~

10. **enigma (n):** a puzzle, a mystery

Answers will vary.

11. **pompous (adj):** arrogant

<u>*CONCEITED*</u>          <u>*SELF-RIGHTEOUS*</u>          ~~*HUMBLE*~~          <u>*SNOOTY*</u>

~~*MODEST*~~          ~~*UNASSUMING*~~          <u>*BOORISH*</u>          ~~*MEEK*~~

12. **zenith (n):** highest point, pinnacle

*summit, apex*

13. **clandestine (adj):** secret

<u>*CONSPICUOUS*</u>          *UNDERGROUND*          *COVERT*          *STEALTHY*

14. **fortuitous (adj):** accidental; by chance; lucky

Answers will vary.

15. **propensity (n):** preference, predisposition

*inclination, tendency*

16. **sporadic (adj):** intermittent, inconsistent, infrequent

Answers will vary.

17. **pragmatic (adj):** practical, sensible, realistic

*unrealistic, idealistic*

18. **sycophant (n):** one who flatters

Answers will vary but may include *brown-nosing, kissing up,* or *flattering.*

19. **efface (v):** to wipe out, to destroy; to wear away

| *ERADICATE* | ~~*GENERATE*~~ | *OBLITERATE* | ~~*ELIMINATE*~~ |
| *GERMINATE* | ~~*PERPETUATE*~~ | *ERODE* | ~~*PROLONG*~~ |

20. **spurious (adj):** fake, false

Answers will vary but may include *bogus, faux, imitation, forged,* and *counterfeit.*

21. **benevolent (adj):** showing compassion, extending good will, giving

*generous, caring*

22. **acquiesce (v):** *to comply, to give in*

| *CONSENT* | ~~*DISSENT*~~ | *SUBMIT* | *AGREE* |
| ~~*OPPOSE*~~ | *ACCEPT* | *ASSENT* | ~~*CONTEST*~~ |

23. **par*t*isan (adj):** biased, showing favoritism

*impartial, neutral*

24. **candid (adj):** open, honest, frank

Answers will vary.

25. **parochial (adj):** narrow-minded, provincial; relating to a church or parish

| | | |
|---|---|---|
| *CLOSE-MINDED* | *~~OPEN-MINDED~~* | *UNSOPHISTICATED* |
| *~~SECULAR~~* | *OBSOLETE* | *NARROW* |

26. **rhetoric (n):** speech; speech or language that is embellished or inflated

*oratory, propaganda*

27. **taciturn (adj):** silent, introverted, quiet

| | | | |
|---|---|---|---|
| *~~LOQUACIOUS~~* | *RESERVED* | *~~GARRULOUS~~* | *MUTE* |
| *RETICENT* | *~~TALKATIVE~~* | *~~CHATTY~~* | *~~LONG-WINDED~~* |

28. **irrefutable (adj):** undeniable, having no argument against, impossible to refute

Answers will vary.

29. **cajole (v):** coax, wheedle, nag

*persuade, convince*

30. **iconoclast (n):** one who challenges the norm or the standard

Answers will vary.

31. **disseminate (v):** to spread, as one might do with seeds

BROADCAST      ~~HARVEST~~      DISTRIBUTE      SCATTER

~~COLLECT~~      PUBLICIZE      ~~PROTECT~~      PROPAGATE

32. **aloof (adj):** reserved, haughty, standoffish

Answers will vary but may include *arrogant, snooty,* and *conceited.*

33. **innate (adj):** inborn, acquired naturally, inherent

*learned, rehearsed*

34. **placate (v):** to calm, to appease

*soothe, pacify*

35. **fallacy (n):** false idea, mistaken belief, myth

Answers will vary.

36. **magnanimous (adj):** noble, generous

Answers will vary.

37. **expedite (v):** to make faster, to make easier, to speed up

*accelerate, hurry*

38. **salubrious (adj):** healthy, wholesome, beneficial to one's health

Answers will vary.

39. **elucidate (v):** to make lucid, to make clear

ILLUMINATE          EXPLAIN          CLARIFY          ~~MUDDLE~~          EXPOUND

40. **dulcet (adj):** having a soothing or melodious sound

~~CYMBALS~~          BIRDS CHIRPING          ~~LINKIN PARK CONCERT~~

LULLABY          VIOLINS          ~~BARKING DOGS~~

41. **augment (v):** to enhance, to enlarge

*increase, supplement*

42. **paltry (adj):** measly, trivial, of a small amount

~~AMPLE~~          TRIFLING          SCANT          ~~ABUNDANT~~

SLIGHT          NEGLIGIBLE          ~~PLENTY~~          SCARCE

43. **judicious (adj):** wise, sowing good judgment

*shrewd, prudent*

44. **perfunctory (adj):** lacking enthusiasm, dutiful, obligatory

Answers will vary.

45. **winsome (adj):** charming

ENDEARING          ~~REVOLTING~~          ~~OBNOXIOUS~~          APPEALING

ENGAGING          AMIABLE          CHARISMATIC          COMPELLING

**46. homogeneous (adj):** of the same kind or type

*uniform, identical*

**47. omnivorous (adj):** having a diet of both plants and animals; eating anything

Answers will vary.

**48. latent (adj):** hidden, yet to be discovered

CONCEALED          *REVEALED*          BARE          DORMANT

HIDDEN          NAKED          *EXPOSED*          OBSCURED

**49. quixotic (adj):** idealistic

*DREAMY*          *UNREALISTIC*          PRAGMATIC          *ROMANTIC*

**50. charlatan (n):** a fraud, an impostor

*PHONY*          SINCERE          *FAKE*          *SPURIOUS*

*COUNTERFEIT*          GENUINE          *FRAUDULENT*          *BOGUS*

**51. tangible (adj):** able to be touched; concrete; not abstract

~~JUSTICE~~          *BRICK*          *GRASS*          ~~FREEDOM~~          *AUTOMOBILE*

*DINNER*          ~~DESPAIR~~          *BANANA*          ~~YELLOW~~          *COMPUTER*

**52. stagnant (adj):** not moving or flowing; inactive

*stale, dormant*

53. **burgeon (v):** to bloom, to grow, to do well

*wilt, wane*

54. **deprecate (v):** to disapprove of, to denounce

Answers will vary.

55. **morose (adj):** gloomy, down in the dumps, depressed

| GLUM | MISERABLE | <u>ELATED</u> | DEPRESSED |
| <u>EUPHORIC</u> | BLUE | <u>ECSTATIC</u> | <u>JUBILANT</u> |

56. **arduous (adj):** difficult, strenuous

*grueling, laborious*

57. **astute (adj):** perceptive, shrewd

<u>WISE</u>    <u>JUDICIOUS</u>    GULLIBLE    <u>OBSERVANT</u>

58. **superficial (adj):** shallow, external

*profound, deep*

59. **nonchalant (adj):** casual, careless, informal

Answers will vary.

60. **catharsis (n):** a cleansing or purging experience

LAUGH      SMELL      <u>WEEP</u>      BALANCE      <u>YELL</u>

**61. prodigious (adj):** extraordinary, remarkable

<u>IMPRESSIVE</u>      <u>PHENOMENAL</u>      ~~AVERAGE~~      ~~NORMAL~~

~~TYPICAL~~      ~~COMMON~~      <u>UNUSUAL</u>      ~~MUNDANE~~

**62. nullify (v):** to cancel, to undo

*negate, abolish*

**63. zealot (n):** fanatic, zealous

Answers will vary.

**64. ostensible (adj):** apparent, seeming

*supposed, perceived*

**65. hyperbole (n):** exaggeration, overstatement

Answers will vary.

**66. requisite (n):** requirement, necessity

Answers will vary.

**67. genre (n):** category or type (as in literature, movies, music, etc.)

Answers will vary.

**68. convergence (n):** joining of parts, coming together

*union, junction*

69. **intrepid (adj):** adventurous, courageous

Answers will vary.

70. **ostentatious (adj):** showy, boastful

Answers will vary.

71. **anomaly (n):** irregularity, abnormality

*irregularity, variance*

72. **endemic (adj):** common to a certain region

Answers will vary.

73. **relegate (v):** to reduce to a lesser status

| ~~PROMOTE~~ | DOWNGRADE | DEMOTE | DEVALUE |
|---|---|---|---|
| ~~ELEVATE~~ | ~~ADVANCE~~ | DIMINISH | LESSEN |

74. **cursory (adj):** hasty, brief

*thorough, methodical*

75. **callous (adj):** coarse, insensitive

| <u>UNFEELING</u> | TENDER | <u>HEARTLESS</u> | SYMPATHETIC |
|---|---|---|---|
| EMPATHETIC | KINDLY | <u>CRASS</u> | <u>UNSYMPATHETIC</u> |

76. **antagonist (n):** opponent, adversary; the character who opposes the protagonist

*rival, enemy*

77. **temerity (n):** audacity, recklessness

<u>BOLD</u>        <u>RASH</u>        TIMID        <u>IMPUDENT</u>        COY

78. **hackneyed (adj):** overused, trite

CLICHÉ        TRITE        ~~SIGNIFICANT~~        ~~IMAGINATIVE~~

79. **voluminous (adj):** having large volume or size

*large, huge*

80. **lope (v):** to move with a steady gait

<u>JOG</u>        MEANDER        MOSEY        <u>GALLOP</u>

81. **undulate (v):** to move in a wavelike motion

*roll, ripple*

82. **supercilious (adj):** prideful, arrogant, haughty

*humble, meek*

83. **infamy (n):** notoriety, evil reputation

Answers will vary.

84. **esoteric (adj):** understood only by a certain few

ARCANE       ~~COMMON~~       OBSCURE       ~~SIMPLE~~

CRYPTIC      ABSTRUSE         ~~HUMOROUS~~   ~~STRAIGHTFORWARD~~

**85. imminent (adj):** about to happen

Answers will vary.

**86. clemency (n):** mercy

~~VENGEANCE~~       FORGIVENESS       COMPASSION       ~~ANGER~~

~~HARSHNESS~~       LENIENCY          ~~RETRIBUTION~~   PITY

**87. amicable (adj):** agreeable, polite, cordial

*contentious, disagreeable*

**88. anachronism (n):** something incorrectly present in a time period

Answers will vary.

**89. prodigal (adj):** spending wildly or in excess

*extravagant, wasteful*

**90. vindicate (v):** to clear from guilt; to prove right or correct

<u>INNOCENCE</u>   <u>DEFEND</u>    <u>CLAIM</u>         DELAY

<u>ASSERT</u>      DEFINE         COMPREHEND      ENJOY

**91. formidable (adj):** causing fear or respect; difficult

**192**

Answers will vary but may include *fright, intimidation,* and *awe.*

92. **meander (v):** to follow a winding course; to wander

*ramble, rove*

93. **dubious (adj):** causing doubt; questionable; unsure

*certain, sure*

94. **prescient (adj):** having knowledge of the future

Answers will vary.

95. **debacle (n):** disaster; absurd disaster

| <u>CALAMITY</u> | <u>CATASTROPHE</u> | EPIPHANY | <u>FIASCO</u> |
| OBSTACLE | EVENT | <u>TRAGEDY</u> | AFFAIR |

96. **gesticulate (v):** to gesture

Answers will vary.

97. **vestige (n):** remains or trace of something

*remains, trace*

98. **ogle (v):** to stare; to stare flirtatiously; to stare with sexual longing

Answers will vary.

99. **relic (n):** artifact; object relating to a saint or something holy

TRENDY          SACRED          ANCIENT          TRIVIAL

RELIGIOUS       OLD             HISTORICAL       VENERATED

100. **arbiter (n):** a judge, a go-between, a moderator

Answers will vary.

101. **stoic (adj):** showing little feeling; indifferent

*apathetic, unemotional*

102. **rescind (v):** to repeal

*cancel, undo*

103. **maverick (n):** nonconformist

Answers will vary.

104. **circumlocution (n):** evasive speaking or writing

Answers will vary.

105. **vapid (adj):** dull, lifeless

*bland, insipid*

106. **demagogue (n):** a leader who makes passionate speeches

HUMBLE          CHARISMATIC          PASSIONATE          TIMID

MEEK            TIMOROUS             COMPELLING

107. **admonish (v):** to kindly scold or warn

*rebuke, reprove*

108. **placid (adj):** peaceful, serene

Answers will vary but may include *docile, calm, relaxing,* and *soothing.*

109. **cumbersome (adj):** *burdensome, awkward*

| MANAGEABLE | <u>UNWIELDY</u> | <u>BULKY</u> | COMPACT |
| <u>WEIGHTY</u> | <u>ONEROUS</u> | CONTROLLABLE | <u>UNGAINLY</u> |

110. **unscathed (adj):** not harmed

*unhurt, unharmed*

111. **tedious (adj):** boring, tiresome

Answers will vary.

112. **skeptic (n):** one who doubts or questions

| ACCEPTANCE | <u>DISBELIEF</u> | OPTIMISM | <u>PESSIMISM</u> |
| <u>CYNICISM</u> | APPROVAL | OPENNESS | <u>DISTRUST</u> |

113. **altruism (n):** selflessness

Answers will vary.

114. **subtle (adj):** not obvious

*noticeable, overstated*

115. **thrifty (adj):** frugal; careful with money; thrifty

| PRODIGAL | SPENDTHRIFT | <u>PENNY-PINCHING</u> | <u>MISER</u> |
| WASTEFUL | <u>STINGY</u> | EXTRAVAGANT | <u>CONSERVATIVE</u> |

116. **antithesis (n):** direct opposite

| GOOD | <u>EVIL</u> | PEACE | <u>WAR</u> |
| NIGHT | <u>DAY</u> | COLD | <u>HOT</u> |
| HAPPY | <u>SAD</u> | SICK | <u>WELL</u> |

117. **hindrance (n):** obstacle, difficulty

*barrier, obstruction*

118. **brevity (n):** briefness, shortness

| BRIEF | CONCISE | ~~PROLIFIC~~ | ~~VERBOSE~~ |
| TERSE | SUCCINCT | ~~LENGTHY~~ | ~~EXTENSIVE~~ |

119. **plethora (n):** abundance, surplus

*scarcity, deficit*

120. **nostalgic (adj):** longing for times or things past

Answers will vary.

121. **conundrum (n):** mystery, puzzle

*enigma, problem*

122. **proselytize (v):** to encourage to follow a religious or political belief or cause; to evangelize

| | | | |
|---|---|---|---|
| <u>*DISCIPLE*</u> | *FOREIGNER* | *DISCOVER* | <u>*PROPHET*</u> |
| <u>*PREACH*</u> | <u>*CONVERT*</u> | *DIGRESS* | *DELAY* |

123. **erudite (adj):** scholarly, learned

*uneducated, ignorant*

124. **accolade (n):** award, honor, praise

Answers will vary.

125. **bellicose (adj):** belligerent, warlike

Answers will vary but may include *peaceful, passive, nonviolent,* and *peace-loving.*

126. **duplicity (n):** treachery, dishonesty

| | | | |
|---|---|---|---|
| ~~*PATRIOT*~~ | ~~*TRUTH*~~ | *DECEIT* | ~~*HONOR*~~ |
| *DECEPTION* | ~~*REALITY*~~ | *TRICKERY* | *FRAUD* |

127. **unkempt (adj):** disheveled, untidy

*messy, untidy*

128. **premonition (n):** vision of the future

*OMEN*　　　　　*RELIC*　　　　*INTUITION*　　　*HUNCH*

*AFTERTHOUGHT*　　*FEELING*　　　REMINDER　　　MEMENTO

129. **construe (v):** to make sense of, to interpret

*interpret, infer*

130. **delve (v):** to search, to dig

EXAMINE　　　~~CLIMB~~　　　　INVESTIGATE　　START

PROBE　　　　　~~COMPOUND~~　　　EXPLORE　　　　INQUIRE

131. **pariah (n):** outcast

ACCEPTANCE　　　*DIFFERENT*　　　*SHUN*　　　INSIDER

CONFORM　　　　　*OUTSIDER*　　　*EXILE*　　　BELONG

132. **contort (v):** to twist, to bend

Answers will vary.

133. **tantalize (v):** to tease, to tempt, to entice

Answers will vary.

134. **phobia (n):** an abnormal, irrational fear

Answers will vary.

135. **antipathy (n):** aversion, dislike

**198**

*approval, love*

136. **extol (v):** to praise

Answers will vary.

137. **resolute (adj):** determined

| | | | |
|---|---|---|---|
| WISHY-WASHY | <u>FIRM</u> | <u>UNBENDING</u> | <u>RESOLVED</u> |
| UNDECIDED | <u>STUBBORN</u> | <u>UNWAVERING</u> | <u>STEADFAST</u> |

138. **proximity (n):** nearness

*vicinity, closeness*

139. **inconsequential (adj):** of little or no importance

*important, significant*

140. **cogent (adj):** convincing, powerful

| | | | |
|---|---|---|---|
| CONVINCING | ~~ILLOGICAL~~ | ~~INCOHERENT~~ | SOUND |
| REASONABLE | PERSUASIVE | ~~AMBIGUOUS~~ | ~~OBTUSE~~ |

141. **desultory (adj):** haphazard, random, aimless

*focused, methodical*

142. **platitude (n):** trite remark

| | | | |
|---|---|---|---|
| <u>CLICHÉ</u> | <u>INSIPID</u> | <u>BANAL</u> | INTREPID |

INSIGHTFUL        <u>TRITE</u>        THOUGHTFUL        DEEP

**143. static (adj):** unmoving, at rest

*stationary, motionless*

**144. flagrant (adj):** terribly blatant or bad

| | | | |
|---|---|---|---|
| <u>OVERT</u> | ~~HIDDEN~~ | <u>BLATANT</u> | ~~STEALTHY~~ |
| <u>BRAZEN</u> | ~~COVERT~~ | <u>OBVIOUS</u> | <u>DELIBERATE</u> |

**145. accouterments (n):** accessories

Answers will vary.

**146. stymie (v):** to stump, to confuse, to hinder

*bewilder, baffle*

**147. luminous (adj):** bright, glowing

Answers will vary but may include *candle, light bulb,* and *flashlight.*

**148. hiatus (n):** a pause or break

Answers will vary.

**149. remuneration (n):** payment, compensation

| | | | |
|---|---|---|---|
| REWARD | ~~WINNINGS~~ | SALARY | ~~JACKPOT~~ |
| WAGES | EARNINGS | RECOMPENSE | ~~LOTTERY~~ |

150. **grovel (v):** to beg, to plead

Answers will vary.

151. **compendium (n):** a summary; a collection of works

~~VERBOSE~~ SYNOPSIS ~~VOLUMINOUS~~ ~~LENGTHY~~

ABSTRACT ~~RAMBLING~~ DIGEST ~~EXTENSIVE~~

152. **redoubtable (adj):** causing fear or awe

*formidable, fearsome*

153. **incantation (n):** chant, spell

Answers will vary.

154. **embellish (v):** to enhance by adding details

Answers will vary.

155. **obstreperous (adj):** stubborn, defiant

*submissive, yielding*

156. **vicarious (adj):** as if feeling the experience of another person

Answers will vary.

157. **parsimonious (adj):** stingy

PHILANTHROPIC <u>MISERLY</u> <u>THRIFTY</u> GENEROUS

GIVING                    ~~FRUGAL~~              *LIBERAL*                 *BOUNTIFUL*

158. **embroil (v):** to get in an argument; to get entangled

*engage, intertwine*

159. **paradigm (n):** pattern, model; set

| | | | |
|---|---|---|---|
| *ARCHETYPE* | ~~*TYPOGRAPHY*~~ | *EXAMPLE* | ~~*INDICATION*~~ |
| *PROTOTYPE* | ~~*DEVIATION*~~ | *STANDARD* | ~~*PARAGRAPH*~~ |

160. **aphorism (n):** adage; short expression of truth

Answers will vary.

161. **herald (n):** bearer of news, messenger

*messenger, harbinger*

162. **bulwark (n):** fortification; something used for defense

| | | | |
|---|---|---|---|
| *EMBANKMENT* | ~~*PASSAGEWAY*~~ | *RAMPART* | ~~*ROOM*~~ |
| ~~*SLALOM*~~ | *BARRICADE* | *SAFEGUARD* | ~~*HOUSE*~~ |

163. **ineluctable (adj):** inescapable

*avoidable, preventable*

164. **repartee (n):** banter; witty conversation

Answers will vary.

165. **fidelity (n):** loyalty

*FAITHFULNESS*   ~~*TREACHERY*~~   ~~*UNCONFORMITY*~~   *DEVOTION*

~~*DEVIANCE*~~   *DEPENDABILITY*   ~~*WASTEFULNESS*~~   *RELIABILITY*

166. **baroque (adj):** gaudy, ornamental, extravagant

*simple, sleek*

167. **voracious (adj):** hungry, insatiable

**veracious (adj):** honest, truthful

*voracious, veracious*

168. **bizarre (adj):** strange, unusual

**bazaar (n):** outdoor marketplace

*bazaar, bizarre*

169. **illusion (n):** visual trick; act of deception

**allusion (n):** reference to something else

*allusion, illusion*

170. **continual (adj):** repeated

**continuous (adj):** without interruption; without end

*continual, continuous*

171. **amoral (adj):** without morals

**immoral (adj):** evil, wrong

*amoral, immoral*

172. **prosecute (v):** to put on trial; to act against

**persecute (v):** to mistreat, to harass, to abuse

*prosecute, persecute*

173. **complement (v):** to balance, to match, to go together

**compliment (v):** to give praise

*complement, compliment*

174. **predominate (v):** to prevail

**predominant (adj):** most prevalent

*predominate, predominant,*

175. **discreet (adj):** careful, cautious

**discrete (adj):** separate, disconnected

*discrete, discreet*

176. **material (n):** matter, substance

**materiel (n):** military equipment

*materiel, material*

177. **affect (v):** to influence

**effect (n):** a result

*affect, effect*

178. **imply (v):** to insinuate, to suggest

**infer (v):** to deduce, to guess

*infer, imply*

179. **cite (v):** to quote; to honor

**site (n)***:* location

*cite, site*

180. **principal (n):** leader; highest in rank

**principle (n):** belief, standard

*principle, principal*